PECULIAR PETS

Voices Of The Future

Edited By Byron Tobolik

First published in Great Britain in 2021 by:

Young Writers
Remus House
Coltsfoot Drive
Peterborough
PE2 9BF
Telephone: 01733 890066
Website: www.youngwriters.co.uk

Book Design by Ashley Janson

Softback ISBN 978-1-80015-248-9

Printed and bound in the UK by BookPrintingUK
Website: www.bookprintinguk.com
YB0460F

FOREWORD

Welcome Reader!

Are you ready to discover weird and wonderful creatures that you'd never even dreamed of?

For Young Writers' latest competition we asked primary school pupils to create a Peculiar Pet of their own invention, and then write a poem about it! They rose to the challenge magnificently and the result is this fantastic collection full of creepy critters and amazing animals!

Here at Young Writers our aim is to encourage creativity in children and to inspire a love of the written word, so it's great to get such an amazing response, with some absolutely fantastic poems. Not only have these young authors created imaginative and inventive animals, they've also crafted wonderful poems to showcase their creations and their writing ability. These poems are brimming with inspiration. The slimiest slitherers, the creepiest crawlers and furriest friends are all brought to life in these pages – you can decide for yourself which ones you'd like as a pet!

I'd like to congratulate all the young authors in this anthology, I hope this inspires them to continue with their creative writing.

★ CONTENTS ★

THE POEMS

My Water Dragons' Lair

Their names are Luna and Toothless,
And they don't make much mess,
Just swim around all day or walk on the wood,
Sometimes though, they are up to no good,
You see axolotls are my tiny dragons,
Under the water building imaginary wagons,
To pull kings and queens to the shore,
Fire-breathing! Oh, how they would roar,
One white, one black, a boy and a girl,
The perfect pair making a swirl,
Dreaming of riches but wanting for none,
Outliving us all till they are one hundred and one,
Plants galore, a tank full of plenty,
And not having to spend a penny,
You see I look after them and feed them their worms,
And make sure their water has no germs,
They have their own kingdom behind glass,
Swimming or walking amongst the grass,
What dreams would there be for them to play,
We will have to wait for another day...

Daisy Adela Anderson (10)

The Pet I Want For My Birthday

Did you know it's my birthday?
Did you know it's in one week to be precise?
"Do you know," I said to my mum,
"What I'd like for my birthday?"
"No!" she cried.
"What would you like for your birthday?" she asked.
"I would like a pet," I announced.
"What pet would you like, my dear?
Would you like..." she began.
"Would you like a funny fish,
That swims around in circles in its bowl?"
"No," I said.
"Would you like a furry hamster,
That runs in a teeny wheel?"
"No," I said.
"Would you like a bunny rabbit,
That nibbles on the hay?"
"No," I said.

"Would you like a cute cat,
That sleeps on your bed?"
"No," I said.
"Would you like a playful puppy,
That you can take for long walks in the park?"
"No," I said.
"Would you like a little lamb,
That can graze on our grass?"
"No," I said.
Would you like a colossal cow,
That moos all day long?"
"No," I said.
"Would you like a majestic horse,
That you can ride in the countryside?"
"No," I said.
"Would you like a fantastic zebra,
With the most beautiful stripes?"
"No," I said.
"Would you like a lazy lion,
That snoozes on the sofa?"
"No," I said.

"Would you like an enormous elephant,
That stampedes through the house,
To greet you home from school?"
"No," I said.
"Would you like a gentle giraffe,
That can bend its neck all the way down,
To give you a lick?"
"No," I said.
"Would you like a big blue whale,
That splashes in our swimming pool?"
"No," I said.
"Then what would you like, my dear,
If not these animals? Is it a dolphin,
Or a parrot, or a tortoise, or a wolf?
Please tell me," Mum whined.
"Oh, don't be so silly, Mummy,
All of the animals you listed are not even close."
"Well, what do you want then?" Mummy cried.
"Well," I said, "If you'd really like to know."
"Yes!" Mummy pleaded.
"For my birthday, I would like a fruit fly."

Beatrice Afhim (11)

Fascinating Fish

F ascinating fish is a detective
A nd yes, he is tiny, but he is wild
S o deep underwater he inspects coral, wondering if he can hide
C autiously he swims with his detective gang
I nside his house, he looks out from his windows and spies
N obody can get past detective fascinating fish
A mazingly, he can figure out 20 mysteries a day
T ragically, he once lost ten scales arresting a criminal
I ncredibly, he knew who had robbed the fish bank
N arwhales nor jellyfish can escape his gaze
G et past him without an inspection? No chance!

F unnily enough, he has never taken a day off
I think he is the best detective in the seas
S *hhh!* Look, here he comes!
H ow will he solve the next mystery?

Raya Toogood (8)

My Pet!

My pet's name is Poley
He is a tiny bear
About the size of a cat
Mad as the March hare!

He really likes to hug me,
He really likes to protect me,
He's really fond of beans,
And he really likes my jeans!

He doesn't like strangers,
He often starts to growl,
I tell him it's okay,
My friend only wants to play.

All the neighbours always say,
"Get this bear away!"
But my parents are very supportive,
The neighbours sometimes come and report it...

He roams around the house
He looks for the mouse

When he finds it
Little mousy becomes fit

He's usually pretty weird
He ends up growing a beard
I wonder if his mother
Would like another

I have a funny pet
You may know him as Poley
But I like to say
He is my favourite phoney.

Rukaiyah Ryhan (11)

Penelope Chameleon

Penelope Chameleon, my extraordinary pet, is incredible and fun.
She likes to play and dance with me and make sandcastles in the sun.
Her pincer-like feet, with their strong grip, make her an expert at cat's cradle.
She also loves to cook and bake and hit the spatula on the table!

Penelope Chameleon, in addition, has a cheeky, rebellious side.
When I tell her it's time for bed, she always goes to hide.
Like a monkey, she swings around with her prehensile twisty, twirly tail.
Agile and adventurous, she swooshes down from the ceiling and chews the mail!

Penelope Chameleon turns brown when she's being a detective, following every lead.
I think she is a genius. She solves every mystery guaranteed.

She sees all, as her independently rotating eyes
give her a panoramic view.
She scrutinises every detail to find out what is true.

Penelope Chameleon has a slow, silent, steady
swagger, so she can go unnoticed.
It helps her follow what's happening. Every second
she stays focused.
She even wears disguises like hats, facial hair and
gorilla suits.
If she needs to get somewhere fast, *whoosh*, she
flies with her rocket boots!

Penelope Chameleon shoots out her tongue with
lightning speed.
Her sticky spit picks up the clues, which she passes
to me to look after or read.
She is cool, calm and unflappable and keeps going
until she has solved the crime.
We pass the evidence to the police. They respect
us and thank us every time.

Penelope Chameleon relaxes in my bedroom spa
when each case is complete.
She likes to have a face mask while I paint the
nails on her feet.

I polish her scales until they glisten and relaxed,
she turns an astonishing green.
She's remarkable, wise and special, so I treat her
like she's a queen.

Emily Gough (7)

Rion The Best Rabbit Lion In The World

R ion the rabbit lion with a pink rabbit body and a green lion face, my pet friend
A mazing, yellow, spiky, furry, long and curly mane, how fabulous he looks
B igger creatures are scared of him, he is thoroughly fearsome and ferocious
B rilliant noises come from Rion: *Pop, roar, squeak!* How marvellous he sounds
I nvisible to everyone but me, his super special friend
T iny wings to fly on escapades, helping people that need his superb skills

L istens with supersonic hearing to my whistle to come home after a fabulous day
I ntriguing stories to be told about his heroic adventures
O ff he goes to settle down to sleep after his colossal day
N ever going to stop helping people, my peculiar pet friend, Rion the rabbit lion.

Harriet Kennedy (7)

My Phenomenal Dog Charlie

My boring dog walks slowly around the park,
Until one day he finds a pair of jazzy roller skates.
So from that day, he was fast, funky and fun.
He works out something: he can fly!
His friend the poodle says,
"My baby has been stolen!"
"Oh no, what's happened?"
"Well, when I was in my bed,
I heard a screeching noise.
Argh and the puppy was gone!"
"I will try my best for you!"
"Oh, thank you!" says the poodle,
So off goes Charlie to find the puppy.
So off he goes to look for the puppy,
He searches high and low.
Then he hears the puppy whimpering, whining and wailing.
He sniffs in the air; he smells a man.
So he looks and he looks,
No puppy is to be found,

But after a minute, he spots the man!
The man is running with the puppy in his hands.
He swooshes down, grabs the man,
And he flies back with the puppy and the robber.
The robber screams, "Let me go!"
But Charlie keeps hold of the robber.
So he swooshes down to the police station,
And then the police are amazed and astonished.
"Hooray for that dog, he caught Burglar Benjamin Buckle!"
Then Charlie goes back to the park,
Where there is a huge crowd of dogs,
"Oh thank you," says the poodle, "My baby, how can I repay you?"
"Anytime," says Charlie.
"Hooray for Charlie!" cheer the dogs.

Gabriella Coates-Smith (9)

Pegasus

It was an autumn sunset of cadmium and pallid gold,
Under a prismatic sky of rose quartz and cerulean which was uncontrolled,
It was time to twist the story of the present,
Not to see the future nor the past which was iridescent,
But the development of the world today,
Inventions coming out from under a moonlight gloom that sailed away,
Carbon full of dynamite,
Weakening and painfully destroying the scenery which was faceless to the beholder's light,
The scale will change every day,
Adding kilograms of our planet's decay,
Or taking it away,

The future looks into his eyes,
To put all the problems where it lies,
Time never revealed itself,
Until it recognised its true self,
The future held its hands with its only hope,

And knew it would cope,
But today was a tomorrow,
And tomorrow will bring sorrow,
Or maybe sunlight chums,
That is where 'it' comes,
The 'it' that changes the world in a day,

It has five feet or less,
With a face full of success,
It is the wind,
As well as the water,
But its flame,
Is not something anyone can tame,
It is in the sky,
But some cannot fly,
A wand full of power,
Changing the hour,
He built Rome in a day,

He is a stallion but he does not exist,
A animal buried in the mist,
He is a spirit and lives in your heart,
His name is:
Atmosphere,

And he solved climate change with just the flap of his wings,
Daylight shined on Earth,
And the skies gave birth,
He changed everything,
Giving a new definition to impossible,
Everything is possible.

Harshita Mathur (11)

Peculiar Peningos

P eningos are extremely rare
E legant creatures that will make you stare
C rossed uniquely, a penguin and a flamingo
U nbelievably glide on their bellies across the snow
L ook timid and meek but challenge them if you dare
I nnocent looks disguise their fearless, scheming plans of attack to protect, so beware
A gile swimmers in water displaying their acrobatic skills somersaulting out of the water
R elax in the sun's sizzling rays, on their candy cane legs they stand taller and taller

P ink, soft, magnificent feathers that dazzle in the light
E very one is a beautiful sight
T ogether in colonies they are found and never alone
S earch as hard as you can as their location is unknown.

Olivia Ludwig (8)

Pun

Pun is my pet,
Pun is fluffy when you stroke him.

You will want to stay with him,
He has lots of fun and entertainment,
When he has got time for amazing fun,
Waiting for his lovely fun,
Ten out of ten, yes.

Adventurous, he has lots of fun on his adventures,
He is loved and cosy and cute,
So cute when you cuddle him,
You will love him so much,
When you see him, you will say, "Aww."

He plays and gets lots of love,
He has lots of food to eat,
He loves sleeping when he has time,
And is not going on adventures or playing,
He loves playing, but he likes sleeping.

He has been brave for a few years,
Because he has got a broken hip,

And had to have a hip operation,
He hates when he gets touched on the hip,
Because of the hip operation,
But we love him so much.

He is three years old,
He has lots of knowledge,
And he has lots of friends.

He makes me smile every day and night,
He should make you smile too,
He can be even cuter when he is asleep,
But he is always so cute.

He is yellow and orange,
He has lots of fur,
He has been this way since day one,
You will adore him just like me,
He has a lot of space in the garden,
And he loves lying on the grass as well.

Tala Ali

My Flying Peculiar Pet

I have a pet bunny, her name is Chrissie,
She's a splendid rose gold-pink, as pretty as can be.

Chrissie doesn't have fur like a normal bunny,
Instead, she has feathers,
All pink and golden, the softest you've ever felt.

Bunnies don't fly, but she does,
But she doesn't fly normally, she flies upside down!

She loves to read and is a geek, but she isn't a freak,
She drops me off to school, "Later! I'll be back by three!" she says,
Zooming off into the distance on her roaring purple bike.

Chrissie helps me with the gardening,
But the carrots and turnips always go missing.
So there is none left for me and my brother, but we don't mind.

She has a huge playhouse which is colourful and bright.

In one corner is her velvet bed,
On the other side is a baking corner where she bakes delicious honey cakes.

On a sunny morning, we reach the cotton candy sky.
And at the end of the rainbow, we enjoy some golden ice cream.

On a rainy day, we collect water in cauldrons
And Chrissie uses it to water her tulips, to swim and to play as well.

On a clear night, she flies me to the sky,
So we can play hide-and-seek with the stars amongst the clouds.

When we go home, she hugs me tight and wishes goodnight,
She dozes off...
Hanging upside down!

I love my peculiar pet.

Hibah Haris (9)

Stacey The Superhero Pug

There once was a clumsy super pug called Stacy,
Who was not good at flying,
She once flew into a pole,
Then fell onto the floor crying.

She also had other skills,
Such as a superhero bark,
She tried to use it to scare off someone,
But blew up the building behind her with her super fart.

She could see in the dark with super vision,
Which sound like an incredible skill,
Not much could go wrong there,
But with her, you know it will.

While facing her enemy, Finley the fish,
She decided to use all her powers,
But she had terrible hay fever,
Which didn't help when she flew into flowers.

Her eyes started to water,
And Stacy started to sneeze,

She couldn't use her super vision,
But realised her sneezes did freeze.

She took a big whiff of the flowers,
And chased after Finley some more,
When she caught up to him,
She had backed him into a door.

She sneezed onto Finley,
This froze him in place,
The police came and got him,
And put a shield around Stacy's waist.

Stacy was now a hero,
All her friends would cheer,
They knew she would always save them,
As long as flowers were near.

Brandon Gadsby-Cooper (11)

Bimblebuddle

My peculiar pet is a Bimblebuddle,
I like to give him a cuddle,
He likes to huddle,
But gets in a muddle,
So that makes him rather strange.

My peculiar pet is a Bimblebuddle,
I like to give him a cuddle,
He is rather cute,
And plays the flute,
So that makes him very extraordinary.

My peculiar pet is a Bimblebuddle,
I like to give him a cuddle,
He's a great snowboarder,
That plays the recorder,
So that makes him rather stunning.

My peculiar pet is a Bimblebuddle,
I like to give him a cuddle,
He has a scorpion tail,
And likes to sail,
So that makes him rather incredible.

My peculiar pet is a Bimblebuddle,
I like to give him a cuddle,
He has an elephant head,
And eats eggs,
So that makes him rather wonderful.

My peculiar pet is a Bimblebuddle,
I like to give him a cuddle,
He has a zebra bottom,
And loves autumn,
So that makes him rather amazing.

My peculiar pet is a Bimblebuddle,
I like to give him a cuddle,
He has a gecko tummy and front legs,
His favourite colour is red,
So that makes him marvellous.

Emily Silver (7)

My Pet Doggle

Do you have a pet that you love?
It could be a dog, a cat, a fish, even a tiger!

I'm sure the pet you have is amazing,
But I have a doggle and nothing can compare with that.

My doggle has blonde, fluffy ears,
A blonde, fluffy tail.

But it's not all like that,
It has a green, scaly shell and flippers too!

Most people throw their dog's tennis balls as far as the eye can see,
But I throw my doggle's into the deep, blue ocean.

She leaps from a rock like an Olympic swimmer,
Nose down,
Flippers straight out,
Triple somersault into the sea,
Splash!
She'd get a ten for that.

She sometimes stays under for at least half an hour,
Then her cute little head pops up and she takes a big gulp of air.

I have to be quick to call her,
Because if I don't, she will go under again for a long time!

There is just one big problem,
At the end of the day, in winter,
I'm sitting by the roaring log fire,
Cup of cocoa in my hand,
Wishing that my doggle was curled up next to me.

But where is she?

Have you guessed it?
She's underground,
Eyes closed,
Head in her shell,

Hibernating until spring.

Christiana Christofi (10)

The Glorious Guinea Pigs

The glorious guinea pigs stood in the spotlight,
The crowds were all cheering throughout the cold night

First up was Grace on the beam,
Then Gabby with her difficult floor routine,

Gloria was next, swinging on a bar,
There she was dangling like a star

Then their rivals entered the game,
Battling bunnies were their name

Brad was first doing complex flips,
He did twists and turns and even did the splits

Bethany jumped around with her ribbon,
And also leapt up like a gibbon

Last but not least, Bella was up,
Doing some tricks with a plastic cup

The fierce frogs came along,
They all were very, very strong

But unfortunately, they go disqualified,
For the fierce frogs had lied

The guinea pigs tried their best,
And put their contestants to the test

The judges stood up to announce first place,
It was the guinea pigs, they were ace

The gymnasts had won a big cash prize,
And bought their friends some apple pies.

Sophia Mulunda (10)

Maritu Monkey

I have a pet
Not a dog, not a cat, not a bird
It's something you shouldn't have
In fact, it's quite absurd

I guess you can call it a monkey
But he is way too funky
He wears a black hat
And dances on the mat

But when the clock turns seven
My monkey takes a lemon
And sneaks off into the night
Giving everyone a fright

If you think it's not so weird
You haven't heard his fear
He's scared of random things
Like dolls wearing earrings

He comes back around ten
When my brother goes to bed

He licks his lemon and smiles
Because he watches Miles

Miles is my brother
And he was fast asleep
But Maritu Monkey
Takes a giant leap

And dances on the stars
Taking a trip to Mars
And makes the aliens clap
While he adjusts his cap

On Mondays, he visits his mum
On Fridays, he plays the drums
Sometimes he goes to France
And makes the audience dance

So he's not really my pet
I don't think he is
But he'll never forget
That I'm his great Chiz!
(Chiz means *friend* in monkey language)

Tomisin Joel (10)

My Crazy Kitten Belle

I have a little kitten,
We decided to call her Belle.
She was rescued at my mum's job,
She's really quite swell.
In the first few weeks we had her,
She couldn't eat without help.
So we fed her through a syringe,
And she'd jump in joy and yelp!
Did I mention she had an eye infection?
Though that was taken care of.
Through the weeks of laughter and fun,
There was something we weren't aware of.
She was a crazy kitten full of energy,
That knew jiu-jitsu, judo and karate!
She'd scream and cry and scratch and bite,
She was very, very naughty.
She would attack anything in her sight,
And wouldn't get along with the furry others.
The cats would growl and hiss whenever she was near,
But Belle did not see them as her mothers.

She'd whip out her black belt and karate chop them all!
With a crane kick here and a shoulder wheel there,
She'd beat those older cats and have a ball.
This is the story of my crazy karate kitten Belle,
I hope you enjoyed it and I made your day a little more swell.

Jaye Sayagh (11)

The Shadow Creature

The shadow creature was a dead demon lurking in the dark,
It would sneak behind you like a land-breathing shark.
Lusty nails as long as eagle talons conjured with steel,
Night-piercing eyes dreaded with blood-curdling appeal,
The shadow creature tusked great snake-like tentacle arms,
Sprouting from its torso with frightening alarm.
Its mouth was filled with great flaxen teeth,
It would wander bad creatures' brains and fill them with grief.
Its nose could sense for miles, stretching over land.
It's ghostly body slithering silently under the mustard sand.
And there it'll lay, waiting all day,
For its prey to unwittingly arrive.
And when it is ready, its tentacles steady...
It would jump with a spine-chilling dive.
Hunting on sacred sea sirens, slithering stingray suckers alike,

Dark creatures from below that would give you a venomous spike.
So maybe the shadow creature was not so bad in the end,
Maybe it was overestimated - just a protective, sea friend.

Ophelia Davies

Messy, My Mad Monkey

My mad monkey is a famous gamer,
In a game of Roblox, he can move as quick as lightning,
Every game he plays, he earns $1,000 dollars,
My great gamer!

We have chips and pizza because it is Messy's favourite food,
Breakfast, lunch and dinner, that's all he ever eats,
He loves curly fries and Margherita pizza,
My pizza and chips monster!

Messy is a mini version of me,
He always looks in the mirror to style his hair,
Messy looks cool with his cool dude cap and gold sunglasses,
My mad mini me!

My peculiar pet picks me up from school,
My friends say, "That's so cool,"
I feel thrilled when he juggles with six bananas,
My magical monkey!

Messy is my dancing DJ Rapper,
Looking trendy in his multicoloured, hip headset,
Everyone bobbing up and down to Uptown Funk,
My multitalented Messy!

Krish Pandya (8)

Lulu The Doggy Pop Man

There once was a dog named Lulu,
She worked as a doggy pop man,
She pulled over an officer,
And got hit in the head with a pan.

When she got up, she was in a puddle of mud,
And everyone started to laugh,
When she got home, she knew,
She had to get into the bath.

She got in her pyjamas,
And got into bed to watch telly,
But she couldn't concentrate,
Because of a grumble in her belly.

Her babysitter, Richard Stone,
Came to give her food,
But she chose to scratch him,
As she wasn't in the mood.

She didn't want a tin of meat,
She wanted a sizzler from the drawer,

So she sat and looked at Richard,
And offered him her paw.

When she had finished eating,
She got back into bed,
She finally went to sleep,
With dreams of frying pans in her head.

Maddison Gadsby-Cooper (9)

The Great, Fat Mr Meow Meow

M eows are the best superpower for the great, fat
Mr Meow Meow
R ight after he gets an emergency beep from the
emergency beeper to save lives

M r Meow Meow has superpowers like none other
before
E veryone's lives are saved by the great, fat Mr
Meow Meow eight million times a day
O n weekends, all he does is sleep, eat, sleep,
drink, sleep, sleep, poo and pee all day long
W isdom is something Mr Meow Meow extremely
lacks, although his powers require him to be
wise to work

M ighty is what he thinks he is when really he is a fat cat
E very little poop he makes is really a bomb with poisonous gas to kill the enemies
O ne person is special to him and it's his sidekick Caterina
W ith Caterina's help, he has enough power to kill anyone in his path because Caterina is more powerful than him, so she basically does all the work.

Aman Rabindra Sinha (10)

Missing Pet

There's something missing in my house,
A dog, cat or even a mouse!
Should I look?
Or ask the cook?

Where could it be?
I need to find it.
Is it in my ball pit?
Or behind the door?

I wonder where it hid,
Please come out.
I have nowhere to look any more,
I will find my missing pet.

Even if it takes a hundred years,
I will find you.
Even if it takes a thousand years,
I will find you.

Yes, you might be lost,
But you're worth a cost.

I will find you, my missing pet,
And I won't give up.

I know you're not back yet,
But you aren't just an ordinary pet.
You're a caphant,
A mix between a cat and an elephant.

You'll shine like a star,
I won't give up.
I'll find you, my missing pet.

Maya El-Assaly (9)

The Best Day Ever At The Zoo

Come and see Kylá the popular peacock!
On Friday at 9:30 am.

You will need to pay £3.00 to see Kylá the popular peacock,
All the money will go to the NHS superheroes!

This is why you should come and see the popular peacock.

You can take a selfie with her,
You can Snapchat with her,
You can post your picture on Instagram,
You can feed the beautiful and fun peacock.

Kylá the popular peacock is clever and proud,
She has psychedelic stunning colours,
There are green and yellow in her majestic, fanned feathers,
Her head and neck are covered in shining blue feathers arranged as scales.

Impressive facts:
A baby peacock is called a peachick.
Peacocks have amazing eye spotted tail plumage.
Peacocks are one of the largest flying birds in the world.

Kylá Chenda-Joseph (7)

The Gorilla Gardener

The gorilla gardener makes gardens perfect,
Other animals would probably neglect,
He saves the world from dead crops,
And he did with his lucky socks!

He waters the plants every day,
While you and your friends can go to play!
He has sunflowers, bluebells, snowdrops and rose,
And he puts them into a lovely pose!

The gorilla gardener makes gardens perfect,
Other animals would probably neglect,
He saves the world from dead crops,
And he did with his lucky socks!

He'll give you a banana tree,
And share it with you and me!
His heart is as kind as the shimmering sun,
He also grows blueberries to turn into a bun!

Now, if you go to the zoo and see a gorilla,
Tell it to grow some yummy vanilla!

And if you see another one,
Give him lucky socks, that would be fun!

The gorilla gardener has a useful power,
Because he will give you a colourful flower!

Aahana Sahoo (7)

Florry

My bird sat grumpily in her cage
She watched me turn the page
My book was about a bird who grew
It was let outside and it flew!

I looked at Florry, my bird
And I thought, *how absurd*
For I thought that it might happen
I imagined it, her grey wings flappin'

All of a sudden, Florry started squawking at me
As I looked at her, I was very worried
I rushed her outside
She bowed down and I started the ride

Florry had grown!
I felt like she had known
About the book I had read
The one I started in bed

The one I read next to her
The one about the giant bird

We flew around town
We went up, we went down

She landed at a farm, begging for food
I brought some to her and as she chewed
She went up to the sky
It was like I could fly

I took a quick video on my phone
Even though I didn't want to, I knew we had to go home.

Summer Albin (11)

Gymnastic Giraffe

I have a pet gymnastic giraffe,
He really makes me laugh and laugh.

He loves to eat leaves from the highest trees,
He likes to walk slowly like kings and queens.

He has a little dog called Spot (who can secretly talk),
He takes him everywhere - even on the longest walks!

With a bow tie on his neck and his long legs high,
He somersaults from a mat like a bullet in the sky.

He performs front handsprings and walkovers too,
Cartwheels and round-offs - there's not a thing he can't do.

He enters competitions and performs with a grin,
He never ever quits, even when he doesn't win.

On the beam, his display is graceful and clean,
Balancing so well, it's as though it's a dream.

Even though he is not like any other giraffe,
He's special to me - he certainly makes me laugh.

Abigail Lockley (8)

The Queen's Pet Dinosaur

Stomp, stomp, chomp, chomp all day long,
Biting and fighting for the Queen's pet dinosaur.
Purple and large with silky smooth skin,
Eating so much that there were many full bins.
Roar! Roar! "More, more!" boomed the Queen's pet dinosaur,
Biting and fighting, *chomp, chomp, chomp!*
Pink spots so very pink,
The Queen's servants stopped to think.
"Please, please! No more!" they pleaded to the Queen's pet dinosaur,
But the stomping and chomping was so cacophonous, no one could hear.
This spotted, purple dino was so very queer!
The palace was wrecked!
The city of London was next!
But, oh my! Oh my! It is The Queen!
She had seen!
Roar! Roar! "Please, I'll be good, Ma."
And that was the end of the Queen's pet dinosaur.

Kya Rogers (10)

My Unique Lightning

My peculiar pet is b**L**issful as he shines.
And most people think he's d**I**vine, like a gold mine.
He's definitely not a**G**ile and even a little fragile,
but I love him.
He's not **H**airy but furry and a great discovery.
He's got an extraordinary **T**ail that shocks snails.
My pet is a livi**N**g lightning bolt. *Shazam!*
He's got sharp claws that sh**I**ne in the moonlight.
'Ludicrous!' he is ofte**N** called by some. Not to me!
He is my leapy, loyal, li**G**htning. That's why when I
say 'lightning', you say 'Bolt!'... 'Lightning!'...

Mary de Mattos (8)

Larry The Speedy Lobster

Hi, my name is Larry,
I am a speedy lobster,
You will only find me in the ocean,
When I come out, I look like a monster.

I normally eat fish,
But I will eat seaweed, starfish and more,
But when I see an octopus,
I feel very, very poor.

I run and run and run away,
Till I'm very far,
Then I look for fish,
Or even Patrick Starr.

Now I am evolving,
I'm showing all my might,
I'm going back to that octopus,
To show him a real fight.

We punch, kick and hit each other,
We both have purple eyes,

I hit him so he loses,
He swims away and cries.

Now I feel very rich,
And I rule all the sea,
My name is King Larry,
And everyone bows to me.

Chayce Cameron Gadsby-Cooper (9)

Ode To My Peculiar Pet

So silky,
So furry,
And chubby cheeks too.
With floppy ears that dingle and dangle,
Adorned with a bow in midnight blue.

You dance,
You juggle,
And sing in the sun.
You aren't afraid to stand out
And have lots of fun.

The mud cakes,
The tomatoes
And marshmallows on toast.
So bizarre you devour all these,
My tummy would ache the most.

You're cheeky,
You're charming
And make me laugh.
I turn to you when tears fall down
Like water dripping into a bath.

Our days are passing by,
And the clouds are moving on,
But our love still stands
With every single second that goes on.

My peculiar pet pig,
Oh, what would I do without you?

Shylah Carré (9)

My Sassy Cat

Pinkie has bright, stripy fur which is as soft as the Queen's silky cushion,
Her eyes are like black pearls and her nose is the size of a doll's button.
Pinkie is very flexible and does lots of tricks like a zany acrobat,
She can do amazing backflips and breathtaking cartwheels.

My sassy pet is a superhero who can scamper as fast as light,
She spreads her colourful wings and spear dives in the moonless night.
Pinkie flies for miles to rescue helpless damsels,
She is super strong and can lift a car with one paw!

At dawn, Pinkie trots back home on her tippy paws,
She slowly dozes off in her cosy, snug bed.
Soon, Pinkie starts snoring and dreaming near the fireplace,
Like an innocent feathered leaf dancing in the autumn breeze.

Rhea Ramessur (9)

Tommy The Tornado Tortoise

One very normal day,
A very normal tortoise came to stay.
Or so we thought...
What had we bought?
This tortoise did not move about so slow,
He took off like a cheetah, go, go, go!
He couldn't help it, after all, it's not his fault,
If he is faster than Usain Bolt.
We gasped in shock, it really was quite frightening,
To see a tortoise as fast as lightning!
Perhaps a spot of lunch might slow his pace,
But nope... he gobbled like it was a race.
"There are scorch marks on the carpet!" said Mum with a frown,
"We need to make that speedy pet slow down!"
Luckily, I thought of something quick,
A special cuddle - always does the trick!

Katy Webster (11)

Supersonic Sloth!

There is a sloth in my backyard and he's very, very slow,
He doesn't move an inch until I go!

CCTV cameras caught him speeding down the lane,
Chasing Ferraris and smashing a windowpane.

When I come back home, he sits in his tree,
Looking at me, gleaming with glee.

There is a sloth in my backyard and he's very, very slow,
He doesn't move an inch until I go!

While I'm going to sleep, I hear a disturbance in the air,
I glance out of the window and the sloth is sitting on a chair!

When I wake up in the morning, the sloth is running around,
I rubbed my eyes, I couldn't believe it and I fell onto the ground.

Now, kids, remember, if anyone has a sloth,
Make sure you tell them to watch them around the clock!

Aahwaan Sahoo (10)

Doggy Boggy

Ami walked in with her dog so thin,
As it was her first day, she could bring her dog Tray,
As she shook, the dog made a woof,
When she sat down, the dog made a frown,
She wondered why she was so shy.

When the school bell rang, the teacher made a bang,
She walked onto the playground like she was trespassing,
Everyone called the dog Boggy because he was friends with Bobby,
Bobby was always kind and talked about his cat Floy,
But boy was he trouble when kids made bubbles.

When they had races, Ami couldn't tie her laces,
Boggy was fast but Bobby was last,
When they had sports, Ami would dress Boggy up in shorts,
When it was home time, they made a line,
Giggles spread across the room when Boggy climbed onto the class broom.

Asali Pandithage

Perfect Penguin

Perfect, pretty, polite Polly,
The penguin was a super dolly,
She would save even the tiniest fly,
"Bravo! Bravo!" Everyone would cry.

Polly hoped that people would be kind,
To helpless creatures, they wouldn't be blind,
One day, she was given a pretty pearl,
A very precious pearl that could swirl.

Along came a crafty, curious cat,
Carrying a big, heavy, wooden bat,
The swirling pearl was his target,
With a plan, he snuck under the carpet.

Polly panicked and raised the alarm,
That the cat was after her lucky charm,
Sirens were heard and the cat was caught,
Taken in a van for a lesson to be taught.

Ashviqha Virochan (8)

Penny Peculiar

My dog is a muscly female,
With a monkey tail,
She has curious brown eyes
And loves to smell pigsties!
She can open doors with her rabbit-like paws
And then ask with her eyes for applause.
She once ate a whole pack of butter
Which made me utter,
"How unwise!"
In surprise,
She's a picky eater,
But she runs like a cheetah.
She's black and white like a cow
And is half the size of one now.
She eats weird plants and flowers
And never goes on walks in showers.
She is very strong
And very long.
When she is in the house, it's like she's on mute,
But despite all this, she's very, very cute!

Annabel Pastor (11)

Gurglebum

A Gurglebum is such fun,
A Gurglebum is never glum,
A Gurglebum likes to lie in the sun.

A Gurglebum loves a cuddle,
In a huddle,
But you will always see him in a muddle,
And he sometimes gets into trouble,
And he likes to pop bubbles.

He walks like a stork,
Which is peculiar because a Gurglebum has kangaroo legs,
He draws with chalk,
Talks in a squawk,
And he always eats using his fork.

A Gurglebum is a peculiar pet,
He gets the vet very muddled,
He has the head of a lion, the body of a dolphin,
The tail of a dog and the legs of a kangaroo,
He is my favourite because I love his cuddles.

Willow Silver (7)

My Silly Billy

This is my dog, Billy,
He hates cuddles and is silly,
He drinks tea when it's chilly,
Scared of the cat named Milly.

His day starts by reading the news,
For breakfast, he has toast and juice,
He would put on his fancy boots,
Down the road he loves to scoot.

Lots of sunscreen he would spray,
Wearing his hat for the sunny day,
Ready to splash in his spotty trunks,
Lots of lemonade he had drunk.

Tightening his glasses, pencil in paw,
He knows maths, English and how to draw,
He can finish my homework in a blink,
He's much, much smarter than you think.

My Billy is a genius and so cool,
I will be popular in school,
Argh! He is such a big fool,
He covered my homework in drool!

Ayaan Singhal (9)

The Unique Unicorn That Wasn't Like The Others

U nicorns are rare, majestic, mythical creatures
N othing else has that many features
I wish I had enchanted superpowers just like them
C ara my precious unicorn and I will be best friends till the end
O ver the moon and back
R iding faster than a careering car on a rough, rocky racetrack
N ever been in a car but only on a motorbike - same as humans, she wears expensive Nike

C haotic catastrophes going on with cooking
A nd surprisingly, she did it without looking!
R eading quietly in the popular library - slyly devouring delicious berries
A lso munching are Cara's friends - the glamorous, magical fairies!

Elysia Miller (8)

Detective Dinosaurs

D avid, Harry, Eve and Olivia were
E ating lunch
T hey were the detectives
E mily, their visitor, had a problem
C atlin, Emily's cat, was missing
T hey took every single detail from Emily
I t was a ginger cat
V iolet was her collar's colour and she was an
E nergetic cat

D uncan Street was their first stop
I ndigo Street was the second
N orthern Street was the third
O ld Ball Street was the fourth
S earched and searched and searched...
A t last, they found Catlin
U nder the bridge, they found her
R eturned Catlin to Emily
S o they all lived happily ever after!

Bhanu Netra Duvvuri (7)

My Incredible Anaconda

My incredible anaconda is the most amazing thing,
He's the best of pets, in the jungle he should be king!
My incredible anaconda has the name of Snarp,
Because his tail is really quite sharp.
My loving anaconda gives the best hugs ever,
And he helps me with my homework, he's amazingly clever!
Some say he's dangerous,
Some say he's ferocious,
But I say he's sassy and a little bit messy,
My super anaconda can do anything he likes,
He could fly high in the sky or even grow spikes!
I wonder when he gets older, what he will be,
I really don't mind, as long as he saves his best hugs for me!

Josh Ridout (7)

Is It A Dog?

Zeus is meant to be the colour blue,
Depending on the weather,
He can turn grey and brown in the morning dew.
He never barks, only talks with a groan,
Is he human? As this is unknown.
He dodges puddles so not to get wet,
Tries not to get hurt as he is scared of the vet.
He never sleeps in his dog cage,
As he thinks he's human and our bed is his stage.
He's a large, muscular dog with pride,
Little do we see him run away and hide.
His dog breed is known to be like a nanny,
I must admit he looks like my granny.
Zeus is the name of a Greek god,
He thinks he's human, such a silly sod.

Neha Jalota (10)

Police Owl

Out and about at night,
Oh, you poor child,
If you're out, don't catch his sight,
Just make sure the temperature's mild.

Silly, old Billy,
Don't come out at night,
Billy, you're so silly,
Now he has caught you.

Police owl is out,
Mouse run away,
Don't worry little girl, just shout,
But it was too late, the girl got taken.

He only caught the baddies,
For the safety of the town,
He got rejoiced for the crown's return,
But one day, something popped up... and it was brown.

Brown was a child that was a hunter,
Owl needed help, so he called a meeting,
Her real name was Haunter,
But bad luck Brown, she was caught by Police Owl.

Isabelle Blakemore

Sammy Snake Is His Name

S ammy is his name
A nd Sammy is my snake
M alicious he is
M ostly long
Y et quite strong

S pot him here, see him there
N aughty Sammy is everywhere
A nd yet once calm
K ind Sammy
E xplains his charm

I nspired Sammy
S lithers around

H e is up to no good
I nto mischief he is today
S liding Sammy slithers away

N ow he is found
A nd he's singing away
M ischievous Sammy is okay
E ventually, he is calm... for at least one day!

Perissa Patel (10)

Techie Robo Unicorn

She is a techie unicorn,
With a pretty colourful horn.
She is very keen with computer games -
She will have her name in fame.

With twinkles in her eyes,
She wants to be a computer spy.
She has an extraordinary ear,
She listens to any problem without fear.

She is clever with her computer,
That solves all problems - better!
She has an adorable helping hand,
That makes everyone want to be her friend.

Robo Unicorn is my marvellous pet,
For her incredible work, my life is set.
She has an agile head,
"That's why she is peculiar," I said.

Angelina Mansingh (8)

Rather Peculiar

I see this is about peculiar pets,
They surely don't need any vets.

They may be blue,
Or even smaller than a shoe.

Imagine having a dinosaur-pig,
That often wears a wig.

Or a gorilla-cow,
That was elated to say, "Miaow!"

What about a crocodile-mouse,
That is ten times the size of a house!

Hmmm, maybe a sheep-buffalo,
That is addicted to saying hello!

Or a tiger-brown,
Not maroon yet and does live in my town.

Peculiar now, very understandable,
This'll be the end, so they don't break my table.

Lisshan Rasakumaran (11)

My Pet Rhino

My rhino lives in a colourful cave,
In the heart of the dark, gigantic forest,
Near my house.

My rhino is a rigid, colourful and ferocious animal,
Like a hungry lion in a zoo,
He wears thick, cool glasses, has deep-set wrinkles,
Rubbery, dry skin and an active tail.

He eats burgers greedily and alarmingly,
That are the finest and fatty.

He is friendly, cuddly and cute like a kitten,
That overloves you,
He is ferocious when eating his dinner,
But protects me like a savage wolf.

I like to have my rhino as a pet,
Because he is peculiar.

Alistair Hanna (9)

Rainbow Little Drago

R ainbow, so neon Drago is
A dorable, so adorable he is
I ncredible powers that it has!
N eon, so like a galaxy rainbow in a flash
B eautiful diver but causes a big splash
O h, good boy Drago never breaks a slide
W onder, don't know why Drago is facing the other side?

D rago is much better than a dragon that is made of fire
R oarsome dragon that's fit for a rider!
A mazing like a star
G orgeous like a star
O h, and this is the end of this poem. This male baby dragon is called Rainbow Drago.

Bernardo Baptista Andrade (8)

Racing Rabbit

Once a peculiar rabbit,
Once a weird animal,
Once bad at marathons,
Once was ugly,

With his ears all soggy,
The wind pushed him to his limit,
All good, all bad,
Life is balanced,

One day,
Running with no hope,
Running like a cheetah,
Resilient, never stopping,

Once he hit that final line,
The crowd cheered,
He proclaimed a medal without further ado,
Running a victory lap besides that,

Looking at the animal in its eyes,
I could hear a beat to his tone,

"When your legs can't run,
Run with your heart,"

All good, all-absorbing attention,
In good shape, now noticed,
Proclaimed as racing rabbit.

Temiloluwa Emmanuel Kalejaiye (11)

The Dancing Dragon

My pet baby dragon is the strangest of things,
He has red Devil horns and the spikiest wings,

He smiles when he's sad and cries when he's happy,
But he doesn't like anyone who goes near his nappy,

He moves and he grooves and does all sorts of dancing,
Like ballet and tap where he does leaping and prancing,

He wears a little red tutu and sparkly tights,
Have you seen him pirouette? He reaches such heights,

Pliés and jetés and performing the splits,
He never gives up and would never quit,

My pet baby dragon is the strangest of things,
He dances for everyone, including the kings.

Anna Lockley (11)

The Very Hungry Hedgehogs

In a world full of hedgehogs, the species you're most unlikely to see,
are the hungry hedgehogs as hungry as can be!
All they want to do is eat, eat and eat,
their favourite meal is the yummy meat treat.
When they're not eating, try and guess what they do,
they play with their friends or sleep in a shoe!
Nibbling on bananas, apples and plums,
not leaving any crumbs.
These peculiar pets that sleep in the day,
do so all the time, except when it's May.
Now let's treat them with an ice cream sundae,
maybe they won't be so hungry someday?

Nicola Muszalska (11)

The Covid-Fighting Flying Pup: Tibby-19

As the world fell into great despair,
something magical was happening that could feel the scare!

My little courageous pup Tibby began to change,
by growing some wings and starting to zap things!

He developed a great sense to fight the virus,
that was changing the world so fast around us!

His incredible smell and vision could see the bug
that was hurting the ones I love to hug!

I miss the freedom to play with my friends,
but thanks to my incredible pet, I will see them again!

He is so smart and works so hard,
I just wish that everyone had a Tibby to make them proud!

Alycia Gandesha (8)

My Pony Pal

My peculiar pet is a pizza pony
I call him by the name Tony
His four legs are made of macaroni
And he's covered in pieces of baloney.

He has a halo on top of his head
And each night before going to bed
He has a piece of cheese and bread
Despite what his doctor said.

Not only is he really cute
But he plays a mean ol' lute
Now he's learning to play the flute
He really gives it a good ol' toot.

He's my pony pal until forever
Couldn't ask for a friend who's more clever
If you wanted to borrow him, I would say, never!
We're best friends, no matter the weather.

Aidan Broomes (8)

Blake The Snake

Have you heard of Blake?
An ever so magnificent snake,
When she was young, she was as small as a snail,
But now she's as big as a great blue whale,
Her owner is John,
He loves a bonbon,
He's proud of Blake,
The ever so magnificent snake,
She snores as she sleeps,
And the whole house creeks,
She does this for weeks.

One day, John noticed one thing for certain,
Blake the snake had eaten the curtains,
She went down the stairs and ate a few pears,
The next day,
She ate some hay,
And then a car,
Hurrah!
Then one day, John woke up in bed,
To find the surprise,
Blake had eaten his head!

William Meechan (10)

My Peculiar Rap-Chick

Charlie the rap-chick likes to boast,
Her rapping is way better than most.
She loves to hip-hop onto the stage,
She's not a chick to stay in a cage.
She's not a fluffy, feathered friend,
She prefers to be a chick on-trend.
Sunglasses, jacket, boots and cap,
Really help her make a rap.
Tweet-sweet singing isn't her thing,
She beatboxes a rhythm with her wing.
She's a sassy bird, one of a kind,
One like her is hard to find.
Even though she's as cool as can be,
I love her and she loves me.

Lily Grace Large (9)

Daisy The Dancing Dog

Daisy was a dancing dog
Who sat on a rigid log,
Singing to a song
She didn't mind the breeze
Or dancing in the leaves,
But she was very scared that she was going to freeze!

She has an abundance of moves
To show off her groove,
Swishing and swashing
Away she goes.

She's an affable dog
Who's unstoppable to love,
She's a Labrador
Who never gets bored,
When she comes dancing through the door!

She has many trophies
And a friend called Sophie,
No one is melancholy

When they hear her story
After that, she has a long nap
But all her fans still clap!

Ola Shergill (8)

Superhero Flying Frog!

Hi there! My name is Flying Froggie Froggoe
I am like a star, so everyone calls me Special Star Hero.
I am quick-thinking and clever,
All the animals say, "He's the best animal ever!"
I have a special kite to fly
Across the wide sky.
All I do is I wrap the string around me,
Stand on a tree and I jump off and go *zoom!*
I make sure what I see is safe,
And all of the animals I love to save,
I'm never scared and I'm super brave.
That is me and the way I love to be!
And if you come to Rainbow Rainforest,
I will be there for you to meet me!

Nusayba Ahmed (8)

What A Cheeky Pup!

C lever and cute
H is daring plans are everlasting
E very person can't help but love him
E veryone agrees he follows his name
K eep him inside for too long and the door will go down
Y ou know who he is?

T he old pet-sitters refuse to pet-sit him twice
H e loves stories before bed
E ver heard of such a cheeky dog?

D on't worry, he is soft and gentle
O ver small fences, he sometimes leaps
G od of cheekiness, Cheeky, my dog!

Nuria Jimenez-Villa (9)

You Know Who!

Sugar Gliders may be cute, but never go on mute!
When you try to sleep, but then you hear a squeak,
When you wake up to chirping too,
Who was it?
You know who!

Sugar Gliders like to climb and glide,
But sometimes they accidentally collide!
When they bang into you,
Who was it?
Well, you know who!

Sugar Gliders are fluffy, but sometimes too puffy!
When you give them a cuddle,
And your newly-washed shirt is covered with fur,
When you try to avoid cuddling them,
But you must when they purr!
Whose fault was it?
You know who!

It was the Sugar Gliders,
It is true!

Kate Kulkarni (11)

My Horse Journey

My horse is funny,
Its name is Bunny,
My horse went on a journey,
While my brother was watching Burnley,

My horse is the best,
Better than the rest,
One day, she went on a quest,
To find the lost treasure chest,

My horse was sad,
Because the treasure was bad,
She didn't reveal his treasure,
But at the end, she wasn't pleasured,

I told my horse to hurry,
But I also told her not to worry,
She found a new friend and started to mend,
But I'm sad to say the end.

Iman Ahmed (9)

We Are Fun And We Like Wertuey

Wertuey is fun and breathes fire
We can head to the black sand beach in Iceland
He can create a campfire

We make marshmallows and play in a band
We make instruments out of snakes
And Wertuey gobbles them up like sand

Wertuey and I like to sing and dance
Our step is called pounce and bounce

He is long and furry
Smells like curry
And sometimes he likes to sleep in a quarry

He likes a fish called Dory
But I like watch finding Nemo

My pet likes to snack on an anaconda
And he brings them from Uganda

And at night, we camp in the tent
Made of cement
With a vent.

Arjun Dudhe (7)

Luna My Worry Dog

L una, my dog is blue
U nder no order, she helps
N o dog does this but Luna
A kind, caring dog

T hat keeps my worries safe
H elpfully safe
E very day

W henever it's rainy
O n a cold winter's night
R ain won't stop us splashing
R ugs are warm, so
Y ou and me sit on one

D aringly, my dog does a trick
O ver the moon, she goes
G oing round but then stops and comes back down.

Alexa Cassidy (9)

Slinky The Dog

S linky is my sausage dog
L ost him in the wandering fog
I love him with my massive heart
N ot always though, especially when he farts
K icking and scratching which was not allowed
Y et he did it anyway which was out of bounds

T oy Story is where we found his name
H e had to move away which was a shame
E va loves him and plays

D og goes woof and sits with me all day
O ver the moon, you can see
G o and have a look with me.

Eva Parle (11)

Fuzz Dragon

Thin, long body,
Very, very shoddy,
Eating day and night,
Doesn't like light,
Small bunny tail,
It leaves a trail,
Except it likes hail,
Interested in pebbles,
It could lead rebels,
Fuzzy fur,
Loves to purr,
Long, long nose,
That it always blows,
Peppermint, it hates,
Loves to hop in crates,
Chases cats and dogs,
Scared of logs,
Also frogs,
Very loud roaring,
She finds everything boring,

Huge wings,
Always sings,
She has red eyes,
Eats flies,
Can she cry?
Nope!
Legs of an antelope,
Plays with ropes,
Ears of an elephant,
Is this really relevant?

Lily Weir (10)

Robo Raccoon

R ubbish is his favourite meal
O ptimism is his greatest quality
B ack at home, he starts to tap dance
O n the roof, he has a dance party...

R andomly shooting lasers out of his butt
A fterwards, you can see him stuffing cookies into his mouth
C ookies are by far his favourite snack
C an he poop out diamonds? Yes, yes he can
O n my bed, he will sleep and he will never leave
O nly with me, he will stay
N othing will get in his way.

Amelia Tena Hurtado (10)

The Rock Star Rabbit

My pet baby rabbit does the strangest of things,
She headbangs and moshes as the radio sings,
She picks up her hairbrush and begins to sing,
She tosses her hair and does crazy spins,

My pet baby rabbit wears a pink leather jacket,
Covered in gems and jewels scattered around it,
She wears a purple bandana and has piercings too,
And she uses the best conditioner and shampoo,

She plays the piano, drums as well,
She is very good at this, as you can tell,
She sends the audience wild with claps and cheers,
Having a rock star rabbit is incredibly weird.

Amelia Lockley (11)

My Peculiar Pet

My peculiar pet is a vog,
A mix between a vampire and a dog,
My vog is called Sandy,
She makes me run around and want to sit down and have a brandy.

Every day she brings a mouse,
I chase her around the house,
Eats from the finest bone china,
First-grade food from Narayna.*

My vog is as fluffy as a pillow,
Vibrant and vivid colours,
Ruby-red and plush purple,
There are three layers of blanket.

She has magenta fur,
She loudly purrs,
Has a soft, velvety voice,
My beautiful strange vog.

**Narayna - a famous Malaysian restaurant.*

Aarya Anand (8)

My Adventurous Pet

How I would describe my pet:
His head is round, but he's pretty sound,
His personality will have you rolling with laughter on the ground,
His ears come as a pair, but they're shaped like a square,
His body is shaped like a stick, but his legs are pretty thick,
He has eleven toes, but don't forget about his nose,
His eyes are bright just like a knight,
His hands are fat, but he's very good with a bat,
He's funny and charming and very calming,
So this is how I would describe my pet.

Cameron Hall (10)

Things About Tala

Tala is always happy,
She is almost never sad,
Once she was unhappy,
That made me feel sad.
She had five tails, eyes and legs,
Though I don't get why she needs five beds.
Tala is an alien,
She comes from outer space,
She is from planet Star,
A very different place.
She has very sharp teeth,
Even though she doesn't eat meat,
Come to her house and take a seat!
Tala is very friendly,
She is very unique,
Once her car broke down,
All she could do was squeak.

Katherine Lompero (9)

Hippo Time

H ippo is my loyal and only pet
I ts favourite place to go is the place where we met
P umas are the clue for where you have to go
P atricia is the girl with the arrow and the bow
O nly if you have found the place, you would know what I meant by 'go'

T he treasure was broken and we couldn't mend
I t might not make sense for you
M ay you keep this in mind, that if you understand, you will come to an end
E xactly what I thought happened, your body is a hen!

Ali Sheikh (8)

Bella

B ella was a very weird creature; she had soft fur
and bright eyes like any other dog, but still, she
was different...
E very night she would sneak out of bed and go
somewhere, I would never know where
L iz, her owner, was beginning to worry as Bella
returned home late every morning
L ike any owner would, Liz locked up every exit in
her house to prevent Bella getting out, but still,
she managed to escape
A fter a few more worrying weeks, Liz found
something else out... Bella could walk through
walls!

Elise Kerr (10)

My Adventure With Josh

Once I went on a trip with my family,
Suddenly, I saw a flying dog.
I asked him for a ride,
And he happily said yes.
He took me to his family,
And I met his mum called Mary,
His dad called Mike,
And his twin baby siblings.
We went to Jupiter to see navy buildings,
We had to go,
Because the monsters told us to go away.
On the way home,
We fell into a pool of foam.
When I went home,
We had to say goodbye.
A few weeks later,
Josh sent me some apple pie.

Nina Kuzimska (7)

Super Sonic

S uper Sonic is good at saving people, running really fast
U p levelled star hero
P owerful legs that go the speed of sound
E nemy is called Eggman and he is smart with tech
"R ip his butt," Super Sonic says to his buddy Super Tail

S uper special to me
O n task when it comes to saving people and defeating his enemy
N ever gets distracted
I ndependent most of the time
C urls down to spin straight, calls a spin dash to destroy Eggman's bots.

Shlok Patel (8)

My Dog Thinks Like A Human

You will never guess what my dog did today... or can you?
He started the day feeling somewhat blue,
He decided he wanted to spend the day being you!
To my surprise, he suddenly talked,
And as a human, he walked,
And combed his hair with a brush,
And ran to a store in a rush.
He bought himself a fancy shirt,
A tie but avoided the skirt!
Whiffles wanted a delicious lunch,
Along with some juicy punch.
He thought about how lucky you are,
But being human was going just too far.

Harison Wright (10)

My Best Friend

He has legs as short as pegs
A tail as big as a whale
A nose as long as a hose
And teeth as blunt as a leaf
When I show people him, they say...
"It's not a dog or a cat,
Not even a monkey... so what is that?"
Just because he's different, people don't like him
But to me, he's just the best friend in the world
People think he's a twist and a curl
Whatever shape or size or even if he smelt like rotten cheese
I would still love him; this is a message saying:
Don't discriminate, please.

Jia Mistry (10)

Ella The Gymnast

Ella is a pink cat,
She liked to sit on the red mat.
Ella had a friend called Mog,
Who loved to sit on the log.
One day, Ella and Mog went to the park,
And they met Noah with his ark.
They went inside Noah's house,
And inside animals pounced.
Ella looked up at the bars,
Just as Noah was making tarts.
Ella was amazed at what she had seen,
A gymnast, that's what I want to be.
So Ella went to the gym,
And at the gym, she met a friend called Tim.

Daisy Snelson (9)

The Takalia

T his animal is quite naughty, but it is still really kind
A lthough it is a bit scaly, it is nice and friendly
K eeper of this animal is tired of chasing the Takalia
A mazingly, the Takalia can shoot fire out of its eyes
L ovingly, this animal is not aggressive, instead, it is very caring
I nstantly, the Takalia's tail can get fluffier when it can see a storm
A nd finally, the Takalia can find trouble and control people with its spike.

Grace Keegan (7)

My Crazy Animals

There's a chicken in the kitchen
A bat in my hat
A prawn on the lawn

There's a chicken in the kitchen
A bee in my tea
A dog on a log

There's a chicken in the kitchen
A crab in the lab
A rhino on my limo

There's a chicken in the kitchen
A cow on my couch
A fish on a dish

There's a chicken in the kitchen
A hippo singing hip-hop
A poodle eating noodles

My crazy animals are everywhere.

Olivia Yamakawa (8)

My Pets!

Inside my house there is always a chatter,
A squeak, squawk and a natter,
It's my pets, they play all day,
With a miaow and a woof,
And... is that a neigh?

My peculiar pets you see,
Just can't sit still,
But what's the fun in being quiet,
When you could run around and cause a riot,
That's what my pets think!

So don't be alarmed,
If you hear a squawk or a miaow,
And maybe the odd squeak,
When you enter my house!

Emily Burnard (9)

My Pet Patrick

My pet Patrick was black and white,
With orange beak, yes, he was a penguin, that's right!
He and I both loved to swim,
So every so often, we would go off on a whim!
Like a torpedo, zipping and zooming under the sea,
We hit the land where there was plenty to see!
From New York to Sydney, we waddled along,
It was very clear to all, together we belonged.
Belly sliding down the icy slopes,
We flapped and greeted the passing boats.
Gulping down fish until well fed.
We drifted off exhausted, straight to bed!

Rocco Pugliese (9)

The Magic Monkey

M eet a marvellous monkey magician
A n extraordinary creature
G osh, everyone says
I t has an enchanting feature
C razily, he can do any trick

M akes the best of dreams come true
O bviously, he's amazing
N o one knows a trick he can't do
K eep your eyes peeled
E veryone will love him and be in awe of him too
Y ou've got to go and meet him, he's waiting for you.

Vincent Knight (9)

My Flying Lizard

M y lizard is a dragon
Y ou may see him fly over cities

F eared by all
L azy like me
Y et he is adorable
I ncredible in every way
N ever a dull moment
G aming with him by my side

L unchtime is fun
I nsects are his favourite treat
Z zzzs after his belly is full
A lways excited
R eady for another day
D ays with him are memorable.

Aariz Hussain (11)

Super Steve The Singing Seabass

Have you seen a seabass fly,
Soaring through the big blue sky?
Have you heard a seabass sing?
That would be a peculiar thing.

Well, I have, would you believe?
He is my pet called Super Steve.

There's just one problem with his power,
If there's a snack he does devour,
His lovely singing would surely stop,
And from the sky he would drop.

Because Steve's a fish and has no wings,
And can only fly when he sings.

Nolan Blumson (7)

Cat In The Sky

C ute cat in the sky
A dorable kittens it will have
T oo cute to resist in the sky

I rresistible to say no to
N o way, too cute to say no to

T o the top of the sky it will fly me
H ome it will come and home it will leave
E xcellent adventures it will give me

S ky cat flying and going *zoom, zoom* in the sky
K ind, cute and amazing as the moonlight glows
Y oghurt it loves and will not eat anything else
but yoghurt.

Jasmeet Marwaha (7)

My Winged Serval

W ings is my flying serval
I n the
N ight, my flying serval
G ets up and flies to a secret place
E very night he does that and he
D oesn't want to stop

S omething in my head told me to sing
E very night
R ight after the sun goes down, I sing
V ery loudly
A fter two days of singing, my
L ovely serval flew me to his secret place. It was a floating island!

Samantha Badillo-Siatama (10)

Evil Eagle

The evil eagle on his jewel-encrusted throne
He looked all around, he was finally alone
The people hated him and he hated them
The eagle vowed he would condemn
With his golden staff, he tapped the ground
The eagle would make sure that everyone frowned
The final countdown had just begun
The showdown would be awfully fun
The thunder rumbled, it was finally time
On the scales of evil, he was about to climb
No more happiness or joy, stories or play
It was time for things to go his way.

Muhammad Haider Sajjad (10)

Stripeless Tiger

Once there was a stripeless tiger,
His rarity was higher,
His name was Tyler,
He lived in the biggest, most incredible forest ever!

He ferociously hunted deer,
He lived in a slimy den,
He didn't live in pairs,
He was no hen.

He was abundant when he was a cub!
Because he was stripeless.
When he was a cub, he was blessed!
He was the mightiest of them all!
Even if the mountains died, he would never fail!

Alinden Nunes (10)

My Fat Rat

My fat rat has coal-grey fur,
And a hairless tail, greasy like butter.

My fat rat eats my dad's vegetables,
And that's a problem because my dad thinks I'm responsible.

My fat rat eats my mum's fruits,
And secretly nibbles on her boots.

When my fat rat eats tomatoes,
His tail goes red like a rose.

When my fat rat eats a raspberry,
He hops around the garden like a bunny.

When evening comes, my fat rat's stomach hurts,
And I can hear his really loud burps!

Nayan Ramdarshan (9)

The Peculiar Pet

I have a very peculiar pet,
I haven't thought of a good name yet.
He's got four legs and he's got four fins,
I found him rooting near the bins.
He's got no teeth, but he's got a horn,
He says he's had it since he was born.
He's got a tail striped like a snake,
He used to live quite near a lake.
He's happy hanging in a tree,
But now he lives at home with me.
Guess the name of this creation,
You're right,
It's figments of... my imagination.

Max Fuller (8)

The Inventing Bat

Batson the bat was an inventor,
Inventing rat-catchers for the summer season.
You see, bats love to nibble on rats,
Who knows what is their reason?
Batson was happy selling his quirky invention to his kind,
And bats loved Batson making rat-catchers for only a pound, mind!
Poor bats were lucky enough to even get a rat trap for free,
You see, Batson was nice to all, except rats, even to me!
Now Batson's good work here was done,
And he could rest and have some fun!

Leyt Sayagh (11)

Crazy Caterpillar

There is a little insect,
that you would never call lazy.
It's a simple caterpillar,
and it's really, really crazy.

When he goes to the cinema,
if he's feeling groovy.
Instead of watching a film,
he would be part of the movie.

Oh look, here is the caterpillar,
he's making a cocoon.
Will he squawk like a parrot,
or fly to the moon?

Now he's a bouncing butterfly,
I don't know what to believe.
If he has the happy spirit,
who knows what he can achieve.

Harry Pearce (10)

My Peculiar Pet

My perfect peculiar pet is as fierce as a lion can be
and can jump as high as a wallaby.
It once went to the North Pole
and brought back a lump of coal.
It can ride a motorcycle
and can use a one-wheeled bicycle.
It can fly to the moon and back
and lets me ride on its back.
It would follow me to school
and everyone would say it was cool.
It can swing from tree to tree
and I taught it to drink a cup of tea.
It is my peculiar pet
and I will not let it be taken away by any vet.

Catherine McGarry

Gummy The Bat

My bat likes chasing rats,
And her name is Gummy,
And she likes my mummy,
My bat likes gummy bears,
They're a treat she loves to eat!
She does not like meat,
As she is vegan like me, hehe,
We go on walks where there are lots of trees,
Oh no! Nest of bees up there in the trees!
Quick, Gummy, let's run to Mummy!
Where can she be?
Just keep on running and don't look back,
We soon will be back on track!

Daisy Morris (8)

Peculiar Guinea Pigs

G orgeous, gentle guinea pigs, my cheeky friends
U nique and cheeky, but nice in ways
I ncredible creatures, amazing talent
N aughty but nice
E xtraordinarily clever, bursting with energy
A gile and adventurous, cheeky boys

P erfect peculiar pets
I nches high, bundles of fun
G reat chats with squeaks, clicks and chirps
S assy and snuggly, my peculiar pets.

Georgia Shacklady (9)

The Monstrous Dog

There's a monstrous dog that lives under my bed,
With three long tongues and five eyes of red.
He can hear really well as he has five ears,
With long, jangly earrings, I can definitely hear.

He eats the crumbs and fluff under my bed,
I sometimes leave him the crusts off my bread.
He's awake at night to scare my bad dreams away,
And in the day, he often comes out to play.

The monstrous dog that lives under my bed,
Is cute and cuddly, is he just in my head?

Bethany Wood (7)

The Lovely Lola

T hey really liked her
H er fur was super soft
E veryone enjoyed her

L ola could fly
O ver mountains and trees
V ery high!
E lla, her friend
L oved spending time with her
Y *ay!* You'd hear them shout

L et's play!
O h, but now we've got to go home
L et's go together
A day to remember.

Emilia Morgan (9)

The Spiky

There once was a three-headed dog,
Who was fearless all his life,
And he lived in a cave,
That had cockroaches and crocodiles,
And it was very damp.
The cave was deep and dark,
Oh, and by the way,
This very scary monster is called Spiky,
And his best friend is called Mikey,
I know this poem is very funny,
And this is why I have written it,
But I am sorry to say,
But I have to end this poem, so bye.

Joshua Afhim (7)

Sunday Sunny's Worst Birthday

Sunday Sunny is lazy,
Also, he is crazy!
After his tea,
He has a big wee!
Sunny has a friend, Lola,
Who likes to drink Coca-Cola!
she finds it yummy,
But Sunny prefers a gummy.
Today is a big day,
It's Lola's birthday!
Lola is happy,
Hopefully, nobody bought her a nappy.
Sunny got her a dress,
But he tripped over and it was a mess!
Luckily, he cleaned it up and Lola loved it!

Aliyah Khan (9)

Glow-Dog

On a winter's night,
When we go for a walk,
My glow in the dark dog,
Makes the neighbours talk.

He is not much use,
Playing hide-and-seek,
Partly from glowing fur,
But mainly from eating leeks.

He lights up my room,
While I try to sleep at night,
Giving off a ghostly shine,
He can't help it, he's just too bright!

It's not always the easiest,
Keeping such a radiant dog,
But it comes in really useful,
When there is a load of fog.

Oliver Cross-Monaghan (8)

My Friend Eiffel

I have a friend called Eiffel,
He is a towering giraffe.
His favourite food is trifle,
The berries make him laugh.

Eiffel wears googly glasses,
So he can spot me down on the ground.
He winks at me as he passes,
And makes a grunting sound.

Eiffel's tummy gurgles,
When he's full of his dessert.
But his eyes still roll like marbles,
When he spies that cream which squirts.

Sophia Proctor (9)

Tiddler The Time-Tampering Turtle

Tiddler was funny,
And he was best friends with a bunny.
Tiddler was blue,
And always needed the loo.
Tiddler was very strange,
And had a small age.
One day, he found a time machine,
And went to meet the Queen.
Then he went to the Viking, Victorian and even Roman times,
Then the white cliffs of Dover, there he climbed.
And as you know, he is a turtle,
So this took him years to accomplish.

Marina Vivancos-Martinez (10)

Betty The Bee

My very best friend, Betty the bee,
She lives near the sea,
And loves a good cup of tea,
Her home is a hive up in the sky,
Me and Betty play music live,
Dancing is fun, we do it a ton,
We get home and eat a bun,
It fills our tums!
She buzzes around the sky,
I wish I could fly,
Up there in the great, big sky!
Betty and me are as thick as thieves,
Forever friends until the very end.

Faith Brockwell-Morris (10)

Spieon

S pieons are wild, it's like nothing you've seen before
P igeons mixed with spiders, what is this dangerous creature?
I ncredibly fast with those eight little legs, his prey should watch out
E xploring through the jungle trees looking for its prey
O verprotective of its little, blue bird eggs, scares off what comes close
N ever will you see this creature on its own.

Isabelle Gregory (10)

I Love Bacon

I love Bacon,
Some people say it's tasty,
But for me, it's simply feisty.

I love Bacon,
Some people say it's salty,
But for me, it's chatty.

I love Bacon,
Some people say you eat it with beans and tea,
But I prefer when it's having tea with me.

I love Bacon,
But not the type that's food,
He's my peculiar pet and I love that dude.

Leonardo Trivedi (9)

My Peculiar Parrot

During the night, my peculiar parrot transforms,
Even when outside there are storms,
With an orange, pointy and curved beak,
He won't even let me peek,
At his super amazing motorbike,
Because that's when he can strike,
Now he's waiting for his sidekick,
Mr Vegan Crocodile,
He is green and greedy,
Leaves nothing for the needy,
And hops onto the motorbike,
Vroom, vroom,
Off they go,
Into the world nobody knows.

Emilka Gavrysh

The Legend Of Zookus

Zookus lives up in the clouds,
She howls at night so very loud.
With three messy heads and Medusa hair,
She's very kind and always fair.
She grants dreams from her gentle alicorn horn,
Flies in the breeze with her furry wings and her best friend Fawn.
She glows when she's angry with a dangerous white,
She whacks you with her incredible tail and all her might.
Be warned, don't make her mad or she will eat your soul!

Kyra Dixon (8)

Bob The Fish

B ob is a special fish
O h, his fins just love to swish
B ut there's a problem

T he fish is scared to swim
H owever, he's really awesome
E ven when he's like a day in autumn

F lying is his dream
I think he did it in his daydream
S o he is out of the ordinary
H e still doesn't know how to swim.

Krzysztof Kasprzyk (10)

Bedazzling Binkie

My bird Binkie is very loud,
She belts out her tunes like a hawk very proud.
Binkie can fly at an inhumane speed,
Stealing all my snacks, making me sigh.
Binkie is an artist and she loves to draw,
Using her dexterous talons, she creates a masterpiece.
While I sit back and watch in awe,
With her incredible instincts, she can cut through fruit.
Katana by her side, she battles through her foes,
Wearing a bow tie and a suit.

Anoushka Kumar (9)

My Haribo Kitty

Haribo, the colour of a marigold is playing with a mouse
She lives with me in my house
We go out to play as it is a lovely day
I look before my eyes and see a big surprise!
Oh Haribo, oh Haribo!

You have stretched far beyond our home
How... oh my... oh my... oh no!
She reaches the other side of the street
And finds some juicy meat
I walk and I see her body as long as a fallen tree
Oh Haribo, oh Haribo, what a grief!

Amirah Ali (10)

My Poodle Only Eats Noodles!

I have a new pet poodle
I can't catch him on my bike
It only ever eats noodles
And it only answers to Mike.

I have tried to give it dog food
I have tried to give it bones
It only gets in a mood
And barks out moans and groans.

It is over-friendly
And loves meeting other dogs
It's so fast, I can't even stop it
When it runs through bogs!

Hayden Lewis (9)

The Mischievous Cat

C unningly, he leaps from house to house
A cting like a casual cat
T ingling with excitement

T he thief found his destination
H ungrily, he used to shadows to disguise himself
I n his black coat of fur, he spotted his feast
E ntering stealthily, he searched for a delectable prize
F inally, he could enjoy the beloved seabass.

Elliot Whiting (9)

How I Met A Star

One day, I went to the jungle,
Suddenly, I heard something in the bushes,
It sounded like hushes,
I looked behind them,
And it was a pony,
I called her Star,
We went rock climbing,
And she took lots of pictures,
Star took me to her home,
And we did a foam experiment,
When Star took me home,
I promised her that I would send her a letter,
Star is my BFF!

Ekam Davit (7)

Talking Dog

T alking dogs are ridiculous
A nimals can't talk, can they?
L ife would be funny if dogs could talk
K indness would be much bigger
I would love it if dogs could talk to me
N o, they can't talk
G o and find out by saying hi to a dog

D id you try it
O n the pets?
G o and try it now and tell me.

Alesha Basford (10)

Amazing Mog

He can fly,
And shoot lasers out of any part of his body,
He always itches and gets patches.

He is a very lousy cat,
But when it comes to protecting the world,
He is up for the job.

The reason I picked Mog is because I thought I
could make an amazing story about him.
His superpower is so powerful,
Wherever he looks, he will fly to,
He can fly as high as Air Force One.

Kaiden-King Brown (7)

Kenny Kangaroo

Kenny the kangaroo does not jump,
He does not spring and he does not bump,
Instead, he loves to ride,
Mopeds up a mountainside,
How does he survive the freezing cold?
Now that is something we need to unfold,
The police say that it's illegal,
To catch him up on an eagle,
All he wears are helmets and hair,
And when he is all the way up there,
All we can do is wonder and stare,
As he marvels in the air.

Eisa Alibhai (10)

The Tech Wolf

T he tech wolf is wiser than an owl and faster than a cheetah
E very day he wears his exciting, epic glasses
C overed in sooty, bulky, black fur
H azelnut claws like sharp knives

W aiting to test his generic gaming code
O range, observant eyes glancing at the screen
L istening to the clicks of the keyboard
F erocious fangs used to open energy drinks.

Damilola-Paul Oredope (8)

Super Rocky

Rocky the super dog,
Cute, kind, heroic.
Oh yeah, I forgot,
He's a superhero in the day,
Cute dog at night, super dog!
He once saved a giraffe in a tree,
Can you believe that?
He is very obedient,
Rocky stands for:
Radical, Obedient, Charming, Kind, Young.
He is only 8,
But he's stronger than John Cena,
And that's my super dog.

Harshdeep Kaur (9)

Flying Dino

F lying up in the air
L ighting up in the moonlight
Y *um! Yum!* My flying dino likes pizza
I t lives in the basement
N o! It eats my socks
G *roan! Groan!* Is the sound of his roar

D igging holes and finding gold
I t likes to fly up in the sky
N ever will he listen to my sister!
O pening doors to see what is there.

Sehajpreet Marwaha (8)

My Miracle Fish

My miracle fish,
It was a very big wish,
It did come true,
Out of the blue,
Little Jesus was born,
With an unusual form,
He is orange and grey,
And is hyper during the day,
At night, when asleep,
He doesn't make a peep,
He's hungry every morning,
But I am still yawning
He's a very special fish,
And my greatest wish!

Olivia Aristodemou (10)

Gizmo

A fox bit his leg,
And he lost his grip.
Ever since he lost his grip,
He has been lazy and sleepy.
Ever since he lost his grip,
He does not climb up trees.
Ever since he lost his grip,
He struggles with the stairs.
Ever since he lost his grip,
He looks for snuggles and cuddles.
Ever since that day,
He has been my cuddly, cuddly Gizmo.

Luna Stevens (7)

The Bat Cat

My marvellous, adorable bat cat is called Jewel,
He does not go to school,
But is as clever as he can be,
He catches all the naughty mice,
And then he sets them all free,
He can be pretty lazy,
And sleeps for days and days,
His favourite time of year is Halloween,
He likes to trick or treat,
Right down your street,
Just like you and me.

Eve Miles (7)

The Egyptian Dog

He always runs down the wing,
He is the Egyptian king,
Half-human, half-dog,
He plays for Liverpool,
His name is Mohamed Salah,
His hair is black and curly,
He plays football,
And he is the number 11,
He is left-footed,
The best footballer in the world,
He is a good football player for a dog,
He doesn't have four legs, he has two.

Conor MacWilliam (8)

Silly Trout Fishy

His name is George, he pulls a funny face
He likes to run around all over the place

He thinks he is a dog, although, he is a trout
And when he finds out, he is going to have a big pout

He prefers to not swim in the sea,
But he wants to run around on the grass and see the trees

He uses his fins for his feet and hands
He tries to bark like a dog catching logs.

Joshua Sheppard (8)

Zelda My Zombie Horse

Zombie horse, she's dead, of course,
She's hungry for brains and any remains,
She dances through the night,
To give people a fright,
I've had my horse for a year,
She brings people fear,
But she gives me lots of love,
Like a force from above!
I wouldn't change her for anything,
She's my one and only, my everything!

Lily Morris (8)

Little Pet

Always following,
Watching in horror,
Stalking, tearing,
Launched out a mortar,
Left on a doorstep,
Next to me,
Imposter always
Wanted to be.

I'm the imposter,
Getting my revenge,
Swiftly moving, target still,
Tries to run,
Door locked,
Took one last look to the sun.

Revenge is done,
Exploited not,
Seen a lot,
Said to the vet,
"I'm just the pet,"
Not a lot.

Akram Karoune (11)

Cuddly Kangaroo

Let me tell you about a kangaroo called Chloe,
The kangaroo is cuddly and cute,
And if tourists walk by, they go bonkers,
They cuddle like crazy,
Little Joey cuddles her or his Mama's pouch,
Chloe bounces and boings,
If there is a pop or a snap, off she goes with a whizz and a hop,
When they're home, Chloe and Joey sleep safely,
And who knows where they will go next.

Lilly Pearce (7)

The Crab Of Doom

Crawling on the bed of the sea
Hunting for his favourite tea.

Two big, bright, glowing red eyes
Shoot fiery lasers out at spies.

Mighty, muscly claws
Attack prey, starting a war.

Thirteen strong, long legs
Grip to rocks like pegs.

The best protector ever
Who will keep me safe as he's so clever.

But the crab of doom
Is the beast you wouldn't want to see on Zoom!

Samuel Lippett (7)

Lizog

L izog has a scaly tummy with a funny dog head
and a waggy tail which he shakes when he is
happy
I t likes to scratch people who are teasing him
Z og can fly but Lizog can eat apple pie which will
make you cry
O h, Lizog is the best peculiar pet, I am sure
G ood Lizog will make fog and sun but it will have
some fun with dog and lizard.

Isabella Rundall

Adorable Kittens

Kittens, kittens, cute and small
As small as a mouse that's ready to peep!
As they scavenge across the floor,
They explore the house,
To see what's lying in the depths of the floor.
They give them a pet and a cuddle,
With their soft, fluffy skin.
As they get tired, they fall asleep,
Then they lie on the floor asleep.

Tatenda Claire Mutokonya

My Hasty Hedgehog

My hedgehog is very hasty
And has a taste for anything tasty!
It can outrun a car
Especially if there's tar!

It's cute and brown like a log
And can bark like a dog!
It can quietly snuffle
And a champion in a wrestle!

Now my hedgehog grows so high
It seems as if it touches the sky!
A peculiar pet, this creature
But to me, nothing can ruin its future!

Pratham Harish (9)

The Rabbit Who Ate Guacamole

I once had a rabbit
Who had a bad habit
For eating guacamole
His tummy would ache
And his body would shake
So he had to get up very slowly

He went on a diet
It was such a riot
As he started to like everything mouldy
He got better from there
And grew lots of fur
But was still incredibly funny.

Ella Phillips (11)

The Crazy And Messy Unicat

U nicat is a cat but it has pointy feathers on its wings and a pointy horn like a unicorn
N oisy unicat is messy and crazy like the neighbour next door
I t lives deep down in a cave
C annot be mistaken for Unidave
A nd she never comes out in the day
T he unicat always says, "Neigh!"

Serena Aikpa (10)

Sid The Cannibal Fish

Sid is my huge cannibal fish,
He eats all he sees and sees all he eats,
He's eaten Mother and Father and sis,
But he's still the most hungry cannibal fish!

His breakfast is people roasted on a spit,
His lunch is five fat, big, juicy pigs!
His dinner is ten big, monstrous people,
But he's still the most hungry cannibal fish!

Katherine Serrano (11)

Sid The Sloth

Sid the sloth is a very cool goth,
Looking real dapper in his black cloth,
Sid's favourite food is deep-fried squid,
And his football team is Madrid.

In his spare time to make a quid,
He plays lead guitar, he is a superstar,
Touring the world with his band,
Sharing his dreams with his fans.

Alexander Turpin (10)

Dom The Duck

This is Dom the duck,
He likes to roll around in muck.

His favourite food's cheese and potatoes,
He also likes staring at rainbows.

Dom the duck is oh so funny,
As he hops around like a bunny.

His feathers are as soft as pillows,
And he's terrified of black widows!

Zaki Chobkit (10)

Loopy Luna!

Limerick poetry

This is my dog Loopy Luna,
I found she only eats tuna,
One day in the park,
I heard her loud bark,
She had eaten a spicy lamb bhuna!

She has a special friend puma,
She likes to tickle poor Luna,
Right from the start,
It made her fart,
And that made her stop, hallelujah!

Maya Yazbek (10)

Rio The Rapping Raccoon

R ound, orange eyes
A nd charcoal-coloured fur
P erfect raps this raccoon can sing
P eople love his purr
I vory, sharp claws
N oisy but nice his music is
G inger-highlighted paws!

R io loves to rap
I ncredible beats he can mix
O utside his house, people clap!

Daniel Cameron (10)

My Koala

K oala is a hairdresser, very weird indeed
O h, how did this happen? I really do not know
A lways talking at midnight, it's hard to get to sleep
L ouder than ever before; I hope one day I get my own room
A lthough, she is nice to cuddle - a big, cute furball!

Nina-Maree Wilma Janson (9)

Snazzy Pig

S nazzy pig on the go
N ever ever naughty
A girl, of course
Z ooming across planets
Z *oom, zoom*, you go
Y ou are perfect

P erfect is you
I t's always good to stay positive
G rumpy is not allowed.

Sienna Singh (8)

The Clumsy Chimpanzee

This chimpanzee, he's very clumsy
Anytime he walks, it looks very funny
When he stands up, he always nearly trips
Very annoying, maybe he should get some new kicks
His eyes are very bad, he can't really see
That's why he's given the name Mr Clumsy
This chimpanzee, he's very, very clumsy.

Usman Abdulkareem (9)

Agile Cat

A gile cat jumping around
G ot some skill jumping up and down
I n the air, pouncing a lot
L oves fish, eating all day long
E ating is really fun

C at loves eating food
A gile cat making a move
T rying to catch a rat.

Malaya Sheen (11)

Super Cats: If You See A Rat, Call The Super Cats

Super cats chasing evil rats,
They say devastation is their notion,
Cats are fascinating, so they are celebrating,
Cats are good because they wear a hood,
They say boo and say you are stinky goo,
Cats are chasing evil rats,
And say they are stinky brats,
Cats, cats, cats, chasing rats, rats, rats.

Dhriti Pasumarty

Marvellous Hamster Bird

H uggable friend
A lways busy exercising
M arshmallow is his name
S trong and adventures are his game
T ender and sweet
E veryone loves him
R eally cute and tiny

B right and colourful
I ntelligent
R ed face
D aylight makes him sing.

Yessine Ben-Saïd (8)

Little Bunny

Hop, bunny, hop and don't stop,
'Til you're home and munching on juicy carrots,
Now sleep, bunny, time to go to bed,
Good morning, bunny,
Would you like to go and play?
What fun! Time to eat!
Okay, time to go shopping.
Lunchtime! Bye-bye.

Rose Blundell (7)

A Little Rhino

A little rhino on a bendy dough
Because the rhino is too heavy all along
But that rhino has a lot of horns
A unicorn doesn't have a horn like that
They have a horn like a corn
But do they like eating corn?
I think they like eating sweetcorn
But I love eating sweetcorn every time.

Zehra Karadere (8)

My Dog Called Jo

I have a dog called Jo,
He is the fastest dog I know.
When we go on walks, it turns into a run
And possibly it could be fun.
He does the reverse of what I say,
When I say "sit!" he goes out to play.
Jo runs with all his might
And soon enough, he's at the speed of light!

Alexander Jefferies (7)

My Superhero Cat

Hi, my name is Pat,
And I'm a cat,
Not to be mistaken with a rat!
Oh, and I'm a superhero cat,
I saw my city from our owner Matt,
If he catches us, we will be dead, right?
Because he is a human, right?
Anyways, I still am a superhero cat.

Igor Genert (10)

Sleepy

Sleepy is a sloth
I love her quite a lot
Her name is Sleepy because she likes to sleep
She sleeps from nine till 5 o'clock
The only thing Sleepy likes more than sleep
Is to eat
She likes to sit still, gazing
Thinking everything's amazing.

Livia Knowles (11)

Penny The Pig

Penny is a pig, peculiar and unique.
Her favourite meal is potato and leek.

She is pink in colour, she loves to wear clothes.
She wears heels, hats and can strike a pose.

She can point her toes and do a jig,
Penny is a very, very clever pig.

Leilani Bird (10)

Dag

Dag the half-cat, half-dog flying extraordinaire
Watch him amaze everyone flying through the air

His wings are soft and fluffy like candyfloss
But powerful because he is the boss

He is strong and brave
And never afraid

Always here to save the day
My superhero loves to play.

Ethan Fitchet (8)

Lovely Unicorn

My unicorn is tall
And the rest are small
She has rainbow skin
And a silver chin
She has a golden horn
And does not like thorns
She has a potion
And a shiny lotion
She loves to sing
And loves funny moves
My unicorn can fly
And touch the heavenly sky
Oh, my beautiful unicorn.

Fareedah Ajibola (9)

Super Giraffe-3000

S assy
U seful
P eculiar
E xtraordinary
R are

G irl
I am funny
R ight all the time
A pple lover
F abulous
F antastic
E normous appetite.

Emily Lines (9)

The Purring Unicorn

Chloe is a clever and gentle girl,
She likes to sing, dance and twirl.
Her wings sparkle to help her fly,
High up in the bright sky.
When she is happy, her horn shines,
When she shakes her tail, it chimes.
As she purrs her magical song,
All her friends sing along.

Kearna Blake (7)

The Grass-Raking Giraffe

Gilbert the giraffe, who made you laugh,
Laid and played but never delayed.
Do you wonder why we have a giraffe,
Or are you having a laugh?
Well, he came to stay,
When we went away, waiting for a bath,
Don't forget, he raked our grass on our behalf!

Elpiniki Eracleous (9)

Tigle

A tigle is a mix between a tiger and an eagle,
It is slower than a falcon but faster than a beagle,
Their big tiger claws will ruin your floors,
His colour-changing eyes will win you the prize,
Tigle's gigantic wingspan makes him fly like
Superman.

Jayden Horton-Clarke (8)

Arkgator

Arkgator is my pet,
When he comes in, he's wet,
Every day I've got to get a net,
To take him to the vet,
I take him in a jet,
Because of this, I'm in debt,
But I don't care because he's my peculiar pet.

Brook Laycock (7)

The Fish

The fish has a tail,
So it can never fail,
It has got beautiful fins,
I hope they do not end up in tins.
It lives in a giant lake,
Which is, by the way, fake.
It sometimes floats,
It's lucky it doesn't boast.

Vincent Herath-Sandor (7)

My Peculiar Pet

There is a magic hamster,
His name is Bubbles,
He is always causing trouble,
Because he jumps in muddy puddles,
He gets so wet, I cannot give him cuddles,
So I bought him special wellies
For my peculiar hamster, Bubbles.

Ava Cave (8)

Rouge The Rescue Dog

I have a pet called Rouge, she is a dog,
She likes to roll about in a bog,
She thinks she is a puppy,
She has food that's very yummy,

Rouge rescues other puppies,
On roller skates,
She has a brother called Blake,
He even bakes cakes.

Bethany Roden (9)

Sassy Snail

S arcastic
A cademic
S avage
S avage creator
Y oung

S tylish
N ever wrong
A lways right
I ll off beauty
L ittle bit of a nark.

Ava Simm (11)

Racing Dog

Three, two, one, go!
The game is on!
Once again, Racing Dog takes the lead in the snow,
Five laps to go in the marathon,
Wow! Look at that dog!
He is amazing!
He can see through the fog,
That dog is the king at sprinting,
Hurrah, he won!

Mehul Somaiya & Tatva Somaiya

Berry's Hungry

Berry the conure was very fluffy,
Cheeky, loud, cute and colourful.
He hated dried fruit,
So he put it in water.
Eventually, he got tired of doing that,
Because he got hungry.
So he made a fruit pie instead.

Lilith Roberts (8)

Fantastic Phoebe

F abulous
A gile
N oisy
T errific
A ctive
S illy
T remendous
I ntelligent
C ute

P erfect
H ilarious
O bedient
E xcellent
B eautiful
E legant.

Kieron Thompson (11)

The Lion

The lion, the lion,
He dwells in the waste,
He has a big head and a very small waist;
But his shoulders are stark,
And his jaws,
They are grim,
And a good, little child,
Will not play with him.

Rabeel Aamer

Sky Snake

S uper colourful scales
K ind heart
Y o-yo loving

S lippery snake
N oisy reptile
A dorable wings
K ing of snakes
E normous appetite.

Joseph Sidebotham (9)

Thirsty Reptile

A limerick

There was once a very thirsty dragon,
Who was offered a full to the brim flagon,
Said he with much vigour,
"Do you have nothing bigger?"
So instead, they offered him a wagon!

Arthur Ruston (9)

The Cute Cat Lola

The cute cat Lola,
With eyes wide shining in the sky,
With hope in her heart,
Will I ever find my parents?
Will I ever find them?
Will I see them or are they gone forever?

Tariro Chloe Mutokonya (9)

Rosy The Rabbit

I have a pet
Her name is Rosy
She loves me and I love her
She likes to eat flowers
She has blue fur like the sky
She is a half-human and half-rabbit
I like her because she is so funny.

Anika Verma (7)

My Kitty

I have a dog called Kitty,
People ask me why,
And when I say it sounds so pretty,
They click their tongue and heave a great sigh,
But then I get into a fit,
And stick up for my lovely Kit!

Nuria Goldston (9)

Yoga-Loving Lemur

A limerick

There once was a lemur called Kaye,
Who practised yoga throughout the day,
Before you could notice,
She was sat in the lotus,
Soaking up the golden sun's rays!

Abba Ruston (7)

The Penguin

A limerick

There once was a penguin from a cold place,
Who slipped and fell flat on his face,
He got up and waddled and slid,
Then tripped over a can lid,
That penguin was a very big disgrace.

Keira Wallace (7)

Tigwer

T iny and cute
I ntriguing and curious
G entle and kind-hearted
W onderful and unique
E cstatic and easy-going
R eally feathery and colourful.

Hannah Sibley (10)

The Dog Who Wanted To Fly

A limerick

There was a dog who thought he could fly,
He climbed up a mountain to give it a try,
He jumped off the ledge,
Straight into a hedge,
And now his bottom looks like a squashed pie!

Lauren Castro (8)

Chick

A limerick

There once was a chick that was shiny,
Who was also super whiny,
He could climb like a spider,
And kept getting wider,
But the soles of his feet became tiny.

Adan Hasan (7)

Speedy Sloth

S peedy sloth won a race
L eisurely, he was not
O nward, he went zooming
T o the frantic finish line
H ooray, my pet sloth won.

Benjamin Phillips (9)

The Dangerous Dog

Bob the dog doesn't bark
And he is scary
Ripping the people apart
Keeping a magical bone
Inside his kennel, he sleeps
Nobody should come in
Greediness is his middle name.

Daisy Ford (8)

Jane And The Bee

A limerick

There once was a lady called Jane,
She slipped and fell down a drain,
She tried to climb free,
But was attacked by a bee,
And she was never seen again.

Poppy Perkins (7)

My Hamster Bubbles

B eautifully brushy
U nbelievably
B ubbly
B londe
L udicrously luscious
E xtraordinarily
S queaky

Skye Jeavons (10)

Super Snake

Super snake
I'm a super sly snake
I like to eat mice, baked
I slide around, I'm super snake
I am slippery and slimy
My colour is lime-y
I am super snake!

Rafay Mehmood (8)

A Snake Who Loved To Bake

A limerick

There was once a snake called Jake,
Who absolutely loved to bake,
He was off to a party,
Where his friend gave him a Smartie,
Which he put on top of his cake.

Mila Golding (7)

The Fish And Bat

A limerick

There was a boy who had a pet fish,
Who had jumped out onto the dish,
He also had a cat,
Who he had named him Bat,
And Bat thought the fish was delish.

Rocco Dellafiora (7)

A Magical Snake

A limerick

There was once a magical snake,
Who lived in an enchanted lake,
He liked to eat sparkling fish,
Served on a shiny dish,
With a big slice of cake.

Kacey Cheek (7)

Doggy

A limerick

I know a cute, little doggy,
His fur is wet and soggy,
He chases the ball,
Trying not to fall,
On the poor, little froggy.

Phoebe Aristodemou (7)

Cat Poem

A limerick

My cat is rather fat,
She likes sitting on her mat,
The mouse came out,
To eat the cat's trout,
Then the cat found the mouse in a hat.

A J K

Green Lizard

A limerick

There was a green lizard,
That wanted to be a wizard,
He practised his tricks,
After a few clicks,
He turned the weather into a blizzard.

Leah Bernasconi (8)

Limerick By Christian Michael

A limerick

I had a pet chimp called Lou,
Who used to live at the zoo,
He was locked in a cage,
He escaped in a rage,
And now he lives in Peru.

Christian Michael (8)

Kastal

A haiku

Kastal is awesome
She is very magical
She has six big wings.

Eloïse Fitzgerald (7)

YOUNG WRITERS INFORMATION

We hope you have enjoyed reading this book – and that you will continue to in the coming years.

If you're a young writer who enjoys reading and creative writing, or the parent of an enthusiastic poet or story writer, do visit our website **www.youngwriters.co.uk**. Here you will find free competitions, workshops and games, as well as recommended reads, a poetry glossary and our blog. There's lots to keep budding writers motivated to write!

If you would like to order further copies of this book, or any of our other titles, then please give us a call or order via your online account.

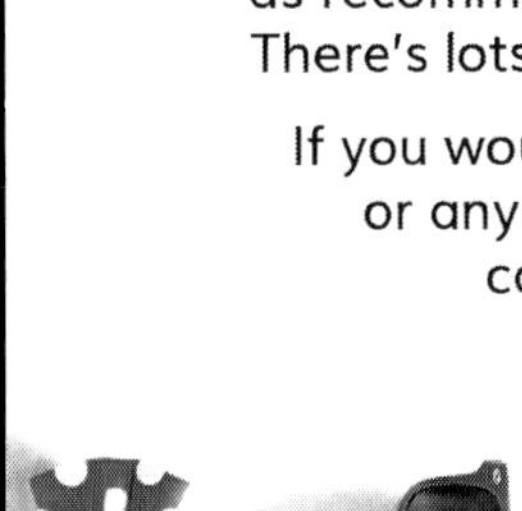

Young Writers
Remus House
Coltsfoot Drive
Peterborough
PE2 9BF
(01733) 890066
info@youngwriters.co.uk

Join in the conversation!
Tips, news, giveaways and much more!

YoungWritersUK

@YoungWritersCW